30 .

NOVENAS

TAN Books
Charlotte, North Carolina

Nihil Obstat: William H. Baum, S.T.D.
                  Censor Librorum

Imprimatur: ✛ Charles H. Helmsing
                  Bishop of Kansas City-St. Joseph
                  August 29, 1962

First TAN printing, 1975. Seventeenth TAN printing (re-typeset), 2007. There are approximately 720,000 in print.

ISBN: 978-0-89555-105-4

Printed and bound in the United States of America.

TAN Books
Charlotte, North Carolina
2011

Contents

Introduction   5

To the Holy Spirit   6

Novena of Confidence to the
    Sacred Heart 7

Novena in Urgent Need to the
    Infant Jesus of Prague 8

To Our Lady of Perpetual Help 9

In Honor of the Sorrows of the
    Blessed Virgin Mary 10

To Our Lady of Lourdes 11

Novena to St. Joseph 12

To St. Joseph, Patron of Workers 13

Prayer to One's Patron or Any Saint 14

To St. Michael the Archangel 14

To St. Raphael the Archangel 15

To the Holy Angels 16

To Good St. Anne .17

To St Anthony, the Wonder-Worker
    In Any Need 18
       To Find a Lost Article 19

To St. Anthony Mary Claret 20

To St. Benedict 20

The St. Benedict Medal 22

To St. Dymphna, for the Mentally
    Afflicted 23

To St. Jude the Apostle 23

Novena of Grace in Honor of
    St. Francis Xavier 24

To St. Gerard
        For an Expectant Mother 25
        For Motherhood or Other
            Special Favor 26

To St. Lucy 27

To. St. Maria Goretti 27

To St. Peregrine, the Cancer Saint 28

Prayer to St. Pius X 29

Novena to St. Rita, Helper of the
    Hopeless 30

To St. Therese of the Child Jesus,
    The Little Flower 31

To the Holy Souls in Purgatory 31

Introduction

OVER AND OVER again in the pages of the Gospels, we see Our Lord at prayer, teaching the value of prayer, or telling His disciples to pray. After His ascension, His Mother and His followers participated in the great novena that culminated in the coming of the Holy Spirit or Pentecost.

To be a Christian is to be a prayerful person, for by prayer we go to the Father with the Son in the Spirit. Through prayer we open our minds and our hearts to His will. We acknowledge our dependence on God, our loving Father. In prayer we bring our daily needs to Him—ours and the needs of those we love, in fact, the needs of the whole family of mankind. Nothing that we need is too insignificant to pray for. Nor is anything too great that God cannot or will not grant it if we ask.

In praying we participate in God's unfolding will for the world. It is part of His creative plan that we pray for each other, the living and the dead, asking Him for gifts and blessings. According to St. Paul, by the reverence of His prayers and His sufferings, Christ brought about the salvation of the world. As His followers this is our vocation too: to pray to God and to live our lives in conformity with our prayers, so that we may draw down His blessings upon ourselves and the whole world.

To the Holy Spirit

O HOLY SPIRIT, You are the Third Person of the Blessed Trinity! You are the Spirit of truth, love and holiness, proceeding from the Father and the Son, and equal to Them in all things! I adore You and love you with all my heart. Teach me to know and to seek God, by whom and for whom I was created. Fill my heart with a holy fear and a great love for Him. Give me compunction and patience, and do not let me fall into sin.

Increase faith, hope and charity in me and bring forth in me all the virtues proper to my state of life. Help me to grow in the four cardinal virtues, Your seven gifts and Your twelve fruits.

Make me a faithful follower of Jesus, an obedient child of the Church and a help to my neighbor. Give me the grace to keep the commandments and to receive the sacraments worthily. Raise me to holiness in the state of life to which You have called me, and lead me through a happy death to everlasting life. Through Jesus Christ, Our Lord.

Grant me also, O Holy Spirit, Giver of all good gifts, the special favor for which I ask (name it), if it be for Your honor and glory and for my well-being.

Glory be to the Father . . .

Novena of Confidence to The Sacred Heart

O LORD JESUS CHRIST, to Your most Sacred Heart I confide this intention (your request). Only look upon me, then do what Your love inspires. Let Your Sacred Heart decide . . . I count on You . . . I trust in You . . . I throw myself on Your mercy. Lord Jesus, You will not fail me.

Sacred Heart of Jesus, I trust in You.

Sacred Heart of Jesus, I believe in Your love for me.

Sacred Heart of Jesus, Your kingdom come.

Sacred Heart of Jesus, I have asked You for many favors, but I earnestly implore this one. Take it, place it in Your open Heart. When the Eternal Father looks upon it, He will see it covered with Your Precious Blood. It will be no longer my prayer, but Yours, Jesus. Sacred Heart of Jesus, I place all my trust in Your. Let me not be disappointed. Amen.

Novena in Urgent Need to the Infant Jesus of Prague

To be said for nine consecutive hours or for nine days.

JESUS, YOU SAID, "Ask and you shall receive, seek and you shall find, knock and it shall be opened to you." Through the intercession of Mary, Your holy Mother, I knock, I seek, I ask that my prayer be granted. (Mention your request.)

Jesus, You said, "All that you ask of the Father in My name, He will grant you."

Through the intercession of Mary, Your holy Mother, I humbly and urgently ask Your Father in Your name that my prayer be granted. (Mention your request.)

Jesus, You said, "Heaven and earth shall pass away, but My word shall not pass." Through the intercession of Mary, Your holy Mother, I feel confident that my prayer will be granted. (Mention your request.)

To Our Lady of Perpetural Help

O MOTHER OF PERPETUAL HELP, grant that I may ever invoke your powerful name, the protection of the living and the salvation of the dying. Purest Mary, let your name henceforth be ever on my lips. Delay not, Blessed Lady, to rescue me whenever I call on you. In my temptations, in my needs, I will never cease to call on you, ever repeating your sacred name, Mary, Mary. What a consolation, what sweetness, what confidence filles my soul when I utter your sacred name or even only think of you! I thank the Lord for having given you so sweet, so powerful, so lovely a name. But I will not be content with merely uttering your name. Let my love for you prompt me ever to hail you Mother of Perpetual Help.

Mother of Perpetual Help, pray for me and grant me the favor I confidently ask of you.

Hail Mary . . .

In Honor of the Sorrows of The Blessed Virgin Mary

MOST HOLY and afflicted Virgin, Queen of Martyrs, you stood beneath the Cross, witnessing the agony of your dying Son. Look with a mother's tenderness and pity on me, who kneels before you. I venerate your sorrows and I place my requests with filial confidence in the sanctuary of your wounded heart.

Present them, I beseech you, on my behalf to Jesus Christ, through the merits of His own most sacred Passion and Death, together with your sufferings at the foot of the Cross. Through the united efficacy of both, obtain the granting of my petition. To whom shall I have recourse in my wants and miseries if not to you, Mother of Mercy? You have drunk so deeply of the chalice of your Son, you can compassionate our sorrows.

Holy Mary, your souls was pierced by a sword of sorrow at the sight of the Passion of your divine Son. Intercede for me and obtain for me from Jesus (mention the desired favor) if it be for His honor and glory and for my good. Amen.

To Our Lady of Lourdes

O EVER IMMACULATE VIRGIN, Mother of Mercy, Health of the Sick, Refuge of Sinners, Confortess of the Afflicted, you know my wants, my troubles, my sufferings. Look upon me with mercy. When you appeared in the grotto of Lourdes you made it a privileged sanctuary where you dispense your favors, and where many sufferers have obtained the cure of their infirmities, both spiritual and corporal. I come, therefore, with unbounded confidence to implore your materanl intercession. My loving Mother, obtain my requst. I will try to imitate your virtues so that I may one day share your company and bless you in eternity. Amen.

Novena to St. Joseph

GLORIOUS ST. JOSEPH, foster-father and protector of Jesus Christ! To you I raise my heart and my hands to implore your powerful intercession. Please obtain for me from the kind Heart of Jesus the help and the graces necessary for my spiritual and temporal welfare. I ask particularly for the grace of a happy death and the special favor I now implore (name it).

Guardian of the Word Incarnate, I feel animated with confidence that your prayers in my behalf will be graciously heard before the throne of God.

V. O glorious St. Joseph, through the love you bear to Jesus Christ, and for the glory of His name.

R. Hear my prayers and obtain my petions.

To St. Joseph, Patron of Workers

GLORIOUS ST. JOSEPH, you are the patron of all who work. Obtain for me, please, the grace to work conscientiously and to put devotion to duty before my selfish inclinations. Help me to labor in thankfulness and joy, for it is an honor to employ and to develop by my labor the gifts I have received from almighty God. Grant that I may work in orderliness, peace, moderation and patience without shrinking from weariness and difficulties. I offer my fatigue and perplexities as reparation for sin. I shall work, above all, with a pure intention and with detachment from self, having always before my eyes the hour of death and the accounting which I must then render of time ill-spent, of talents unemployed, of good undone, and of empty pride in success, which is so fatal to the world of God.

For Jesus through Mary, all in imitation of you, good St. Joseph. This shall be my motto in life and in death. Amen.

Prayer to One's Patron or Any Saint

GLORIOUS SAINT N (my beloved patron), you served God in humility and confidence on earth. Now you enjoy His beatific vision in Heaven. You persevered till death and gained the crown of eternal life. Remember now the dangers and confusion and anguish that surround me and intercede for me in my needs and troubles, especially . . . Amen.

To St. Michael, the Archangel

GLORIOUS ST. MICHAEL, guardian and defender of the Church of Jesus Christ, come to the assistance of His followers, against whom the powers of Hell are unchained. Guard with speical care our Holy Father, the Pope, and our bishops, priests, all our religious and lay people, and especially the children.

St. Michael, watch over us during life, defend us againt the assaults of the demon, and assist us especially at the hour of death. Help us achieve the happiness of beholding

God face to face for all eternity. Amen.

St. Michael, intercede for me with God in all my necessities, especially (name it). Obtain for me a favorable outcome in the matter I recommend to you. Mighty prince of the heavenly host, and victor over rebellios spirits, remember me for I am weak and sinful and so prone to pride and ambition. Be for me, I pray, my powerful aid in temptation and difficulty; and above all do not forake me in my last struggle with the powers of evil. Amen.

To St. Raphael, The Archangel

GLORIOUS ARCHANGEL St. Raphael, great prince of the heavenly court, you are illustrious for your gifts of wisdom and grace. You are a guide of those who journey by land or sea or air, consoler of the afflicted, and refuge of sinners. I beg you, assist me in all my needs and in all the sufferings of this life, as once you helped the young Tobias on his travels. Because you are the "medicine of God," I humbly pray you to heal the many infirmities of my soul and the ills that afflict my body. I especially ask of you the favor (name it) and the great grace of purity to prepare me to be the temple of the Holy Spirit. Amen.

St. Raphael, of the glorious seven
　　who stand
Before the throne of Him who lives
　　and reigns.
Angel of health, the Lord has filled
　　your hand
With balm from Heaven to soothe
　　or cure our pains.
Heal or cure the victim of diseases,
And guide our steps when doubtful
　　of our ways.

To the Holy Angels

BLESS THE LORD, all you His angels. You who are mighty in strength and do His will, intercede for me at the throne of God. By your unceasing watchfulness protect me in every danger of soul and body. Obtain for me the grace of final perseverance, so that after this life I may be admitted to your glorious company and with you may sing the praises of God for all eternity.

All you holy angels and archangels, thrones and dominations, principalities and powers and virtues of heaven, cherubim and seraphim, and especially you, my dear guardian angel, intercede for me and obtain for me the special favor I now ask (mention it).

Glory be to the Father. . . .

To Good St. Anne

GLORIOUS ST. ANNE, we think of you as filled with compassion for those who invoke you and with love for those who suffer. Heavily laden with the weight of my troubles, I cast myself at your feet and humbly beg of you to take the present affair which I commend to you under your special protection (name it).

Deign to commend it to your daughter, our Blessed Lady, and lay it before the throne of Jesus, so that He may bring it to a happy conclusion. Cease not to intercede for me until my request is granted. Above all, obtain for me the grace of one day beholding my God face to face. With you and Mary and all the saints, may I praise and bless Him for all eternity. Amen.

Good St. Anne, mother of her who is our life, our sweetness and our hope, pray for me.

To St. Anthony, The Wonder-Worker

In Any Need

ST. ANTHONY, you are glorious for your miracles and for the condescension of Jesus who came as a little child to lie in your arms. Obtain for me from His bounty the grace which I ardently desire. You were so compassionate toward sinners, do not regard my unworthiness. Let the glory of God be magnified by you in connection with the particular request that I earnestly present to you (name it).

As a pledge of my gratitude I promise to live more faithfully in accordance with the teachings of the Church, and to be devoted to the service of the poor whom you loved and still love so greatly. Bless this resolution of mine that I may be faithful to it until death.

St. Anthony, consoler of all the afflicted, pray for me.

St. Anthony, helper of all who invoke you, pray for me.

St. Anthony, whom the Infant Jesus loved and honored so much, pray for me.

To Find a Lost Article

ST. ANTHONY, perfect imitator of Jesus, who received from God the special power of restoring lost things, grant that I may find. . . which has been lost. At least restore to me peace and tranquillity of mind, the loss of which has afflicted me even more than my material loss. To this favor I ask another of you: that I may always remain in possession of the true good that is God. Let me rather lose all things than lose God, my supreme good. Let me never suffer the loss of my greatest treasure, eternal life with God. Amen.

To St. Anthony Mary Claret

Helper of those suffering from cancer, heart trouble, and other serious ailments of soul and body.

ST. ANTHONY MARY CLARET, during your life on earth you often comforted the afflicted and showed such tender love and compassion for the sick and sinful. Intercede for me now that you rejoice in the reward of your virtues in heavenly glory. Look with pity on me (or on the person afflicted or whose conversion is desired) and grant my prayer, if such be the will of God. Make my troubles your own. Speak a word for me to the Immaculate Heart of Mary to obtain by her powerful intercession the grace I yearn for so ardently, and a blessing to strengthen me during life, assist me at the hour of death, and lead me to a happy eternity. Amen.

To St. Benedict

GLORIOUS ST. BENEDICT, sublime model of virtue, pure vessel of God's grace! Behold me humbly kneeling at your feet. I implore you in your loving kindness to pray for me before the throne of God. To you I have recourse in the dangers that daily surround me. Shield me against my selfishness and my indifference to God and to my neighbor. Inspire me to imitate you in all things. May your blessing be with me always, so that I may see and serve Christ in others and work for His kingdom.

Graciously obtain for me from God those favors and graces which I need so much in the trials, miseries and afflictions of life. Your heart was always full of love, compassion and mercy toward those who were afflicted or troubled in any way. You never dismissed without consolation and assistance anyone who had recourse to you. I therefore invoke your powerful intercession, confident in the hope that you will hear my prayers and obtain for me the special grace and favor I earnestly implore (name it).

Help me, great St. Benedict, to live and die as a faithful child of God, to run in the sweetness of His loving will and to attain the eternal happiness of heaven. Amen.

The Jubilee Medal of St. Benedict is a sacramental of the Church. Favors obtained through its devout use must be ascribed to the merits of Christ, the merits of St. Benedict, the blessing of the Church, and the faith of the one using it.

Latin inscriptions, front: "May his presence protect us in the hour of death." *Reverse:* CSPB, Cross of the holy father Benedict. *Letters signify:* "May the holy cross be my light; let not the dragon be my guide." *Margin:* "Be gone, Satan! Suggest not vain things. The cup you offer me is evil. Drink your own poison."

To St. Dymphna

For the Mentally Afflicted

O GOD, we humbly beseech You through Your servant, St. Dymphna, who sealed with her blood the love she bore You, to grant relief to those who suffer from mental afflictions and nervous disorders, especially . . .

St. Dymphna, helper of the mentally afflicted, pray for us.

Glory be to the Father . . .

To St. Jude the Apostle

G LORIOUS APOSTLE, ST. JUDE Thaddeus, I salute you through the Sacred Heart of Jesus. Through His Heart I praise and thank God for all the graces He has bestowed upon you. I implore you, through His love to look upon me with compassion. Do not despise my poor prayer. Do not let my trust be confounded! God has granted to you the privilege of aiding mankind in the most desperate cases. Oh, come to my aid that

I may praise the mercies of God! All my life I will be your grateful client until I can thank you in heaven. Amen.

St. Jude, pray for us,
And for all who invoke your aid.

Novena of Grace in Honor of St. Francis Xavier

GREAT ST. FRANCIS, well beloved and full of charity, in union with you I reverently adore the Divine Majesty. I give thanks to God for the singular gifts of grace bestowed on you in life and of glory after death, and I beg of you, with all the affection of my heart, by your powerful intercession, obtain for me the grace to live a holy life and die a holy death. I beg you to obtain for me (here mention special spiritual or temporal favors); but if what I ask is not for the glory of God and for my well-being, obtain for me, I beseech you, what will more certainly attain these ends. Amen.

Our Father, Hail Mary, Glory be.

To St. Gerard

For an Expectant Mother

GREAT ST. GERARD, beloved servant of Jesus Christ, you are a perfect imitator of our meek and humble Savior, and a devoted child of the Mother of God. Enkindle in my heart one spark of that heavenly fire of charity that glowed in yours and made you a beacon of love.

Glorious St. Gerard, like your divine Master you bore without murmur or complaint the calumnies of wicked men when falsely accused of crime, and you have been raised up by God as the patron and protector of expectant mothers. Preserve me from dangers, and shield the child I now carry. Pray that my baby may be brought safely to the light of day and receive the sacrament of baptism.

Hail, Mary . . .

For Motherhood or for
Some Other Special Favor

*(St. Gerard is also invoked as the
patron of a good confession.)*

MOST BLESSED TRINITY, I, Your child, thank You for all the gifts and privileges which You granted to St. Gerard, especially for those virtues with which You adorned him on earth and the glory which You now impart to him in heaven. Accomplish Your work, Oh Lord, so that Your kingdom may come about on earth. Through his merits, in union with those of Jesus and Mary, grant me the grace for which I ask . . .

And you, my powerful intercessor, St. Gerard, always so ready to help those who have recourse to you, pray for me. Come before the throne of Divine Mercy and do not leave without being heard. To you I confide this important and urgent affair. . . . Graciously take my cause in hand and do not let me end this novena without having experienced in some way the effects of your intercession. Amen.

To St. Lucy

ST. LUCY, your beautiful name signifies light. By the light of faith which God bestowed upon you, increase and preserve this light in my soul so that I may avoid evil, be zealous in the performance of good works, and abhor nothing so much as the blindness and the darkness of evil and of sin.

By your intercession with God, obtain for me perfect vision for my bodily eyes and the grace to use them for God's greater honor and glory and the salvation of all men.

St. Lucy, virgin and martyr, hear my prayers and obtain my petitions. Amen.

To St. Maria Goretti

ST. MARIA GORETTI, strengthened by God's grace, you did not hesitate, even at the age of eleven, to sacrifice life itself to defend your virginal purity. Look graciously on the unhappy human race that has strayed far from the path of eternal salvation. Teach us all, and especially our youth, the courage and promptness that will help us avoid anything that could offend Jesus. Obtain for me a great horror of sin, so that I may live a holy life on earth and win eternal glory in heaven. Amen.

Our Father, Hail, Mary, Glory be.

To St. Peregrine, "The Cancer Saint"

GLORIOUS WONDER-WORKER, St. Peregrine, you answered the divine call with a ready spirit, and forsook all the comforts of a life of ease and all the empty honors of the world to dedicate yourself to God in the Order of His holy Mother. You labored manfully for the salvation of souls. In union with Jesus crucified, you endured painful sufferings with such patience as to deserve to be healed miraculously of an incurable cancer in your leg by a touch of His divine hand. Obtain for me the grace to answer every call of God and to fulfill His will in all the events of life. Enkindle in my heart a consuming zeal for the salvation of all men. Deliver me from the infirmities that afflict my body (especially . . .). Obtain for me also a perfect resignation to the sufferings it may please God to send me, so that, imitating our crucified Savior and His sorrowful Mother, I may merit eternal glory in heaven.

St. Peregrine, pray for me and for all who invoke your aid.

Prayer to St. Pius X

GLORIOUS POPE of the Eucharist, St. Pius X, you sought "to restore all things in Christ." Obtain for me a true love of Jesus so that I may live only for Him. Help me to acquire a lively fervor and a sincere will to strive for sanctity of life, and that I may avail myself of the riches of the Holy Eucharist in sacrifice and sacrament. By your love for Mary, mother and queen of all, inflame my heart with tender devotion to her.

Blessed model of the priesthood, obtain for us holy, dedicated priests, and increase vocations to the religious life. Dispel confusion and hatred and anxiety, and incline our hearts to peace and concord, so that all nations will place themselves under the sweet reign of Christ. Amen.

St. Pius X, pray for me, (mention any particular intention).

Novena to St. Rita

Helper of the hopeless

HOLY PATRONESS of those in need, St. Rita, you were humble, pure and patient. Your pleadings with your divine Spouse are irresistible, so please obtain for me from our risen Jesus the request I make of you (mention it). Be kind to me for the greater glory of God, and I shall honor you and sing your praises forever.

Glorious St. Rita, you miraculously participated in the sorrowful passion of our Lord Jesus Christ. Obtain for me now the grace to suffer with resignation the troubles of this life, and protect me in all my needs. Amen.

Our Father, Hail, Mary, Glory be to the Father . . .

To St. Therese of the Child Jesus, "The Little Flower"

I GREET YOU, St. Therese of the Child Jesus, lily of purity, ornament and glory of Christianity. I greet you, great Saint, seraph of divine love. I rejoice at the favors our blessed Lord Jesus has liberally bestowed on you. In humility and confidence I ask you to help me, for I know that God has given you love and pity as well as power. Then, behold my distress, my anxiety, my fears. Tell Him my wants. Your requests will crown my petition with success, will fill me with joy. Remember your promise to do good on earth. Please obtain for me from God the graces I hope for from the infinite goodness of our blessed Lord, especially . . . Amen.

To the Holy Souls in Purgatory

O HOLY SOULS in purgatory, you are the certain heirs of heaven. You are most dear to Jesus as the trophies of His Precious Blood and to Mary, mother

of mercy. Obtain for me through your intercession the grace to lead a holy life, to die
a happy death and to attain to the blessed-
ness of eternity in heaven.

Dear suffering souls, who long to be
delivered in order to praise and glorify God
in heaven, by your unfailing pity help me
in the needs which distress me at this time,
particularly . . . so that I may obtain relief
and assistance from God.

In gratitude for your intercession I offer
to God in your behalf the satisfactory merits of my prayer and work, my joys and sufferings of this day (week, month, or whatever
space of time you wish to designate).

Assist at Mass and have a Mass offered for them, if
possible. Offerings of the Precious Blood and the Way of
the Cross are also powerful means of helping them and
obtaining their help.